CALMING SUCCULENTS AND CACTI COLORING BOOK

COLOR THERAPY

M. CRYPTKEEPER

ISBN: 1974461580

ISBN-13: 978-1974461585

INTRODUCTION

COLOR IN VARIOUS CRUDELY SKETCHED CALMING SUCCULENTS AND CACTI.

EACH PAGE IS DOUBLED SO YOU'LL BE ABLE TO KEEP AN ORIGINAL OUTLINE TO SCAN OR COPY FOR FUTURE COLORING USE.

PERFECT FOR PEOPLE WHO LOVE PLANTS.

HAND DRAWN ILLUSTRATIONS BY M. CRYPTKEEPER.

CONTENTS

WHAT IS A SUCCULENT?

A GENERAL DEFINITION OF SUCCULENTS IS: A PLANT WITH THICK, FLESHY AND SWOLLEN STEMS AND OR LEAVES. THEY'RE ADAPTED TO DRY ENVIRONMENTS.

WHAT IS A CACTUS?

CACTI GROW IN A WIDE RANGE OF SHAPES AND SIZES. MOST CACTI LIVE IN DROUGHT HABITATS. MANY LIVE IN EXTREME DRY ENVIRONMENTS.

MOST CACTI ARE SUCCULENTS, MEANING THEY HAVE THICKENED, FLESHY PARTS ADAPTED TO STORE WATER. UNLIKE SOME SUCCULENTS, THE STEM IS THE ONLY PART OF MOST CACTI WHERE THIS PROCESS TAKES PLACE.

This page has been kept blank to prevent pen BLEEDING.

This page has been kept blank to prevent pen **BLEEDING.**

This page has been kept blank to prevent pen BLEEDING.

This page has been kept blank to prevent pen BLEEDING.

This page has been kept blank to prevent pen BLEEDING.

This page has been kept blank to prevent pen BLEEDING.

This page has been kept blank to prevent pen BLEEDING.

This page has been kept blank to prevent pen **BLEEDING.**

This page has been kept blank to prevent pen BLEEDING.

This page has been kept blank to prevent pen BLEEDING.

This page has been kept blank to prevent pen BLEEDING.

This page has been kept blank to prevent pen BLEEDING.

This page has been kept blank to prevent pen BLEEDING.

This page has been kept blank to prevent pen BLEEDING.

This page has been kept blank to prevent pen BLEEDING.

This page has been kept blank to prevent pen BLEEDING.

This page has been kept blank to prevent pen BLEEDING.

This page has been kept blank to prevent pen **BLEEDING.**

This page has been kept blank to prevent pen BLEEDING.

This page has been kept blank to prevent pen BLEEDING.

THANK YOU FOR SUPPORTING PUMPKIN
PUBLICATIONS, I HOPE YOU'RE NOT TOO SPOOKED.

PLEASE LEAVE A REVIEW IF POSSIBLE, AS YOUR
FEEDBACK IS MUCH APPRECIATED.

ABOUT THE AUTHOR

M. CRYPTKEEPER IS A GRADUATED ART STUDENT
BASED IN THE UNITED KINGDOM (LONDON ESSEX).
WITH A PASSION FOR ILLUSTRATION AND HORROR
IT ONLY MADE SENSE FOR HER TO START
PUMPKIN PUBLICATIONS: AN INDIE BOOK COMPANY
THAT SPECIALIZES IN MODERN HORROR FOLK
TALES AND HAND DRAWN COLOUR THERAPY.
HER QUIRKY STYLE INSTANTLY TRANSLATES
INTO HER BOOKS CREATING A TRULY IMMERSIVE
EXPERIENCE.

Made in the USA
Las Vegas, NV
23 October 2024

10327866R00031